Conversations

on

The Sound of Glass
Karen White

By dailyBooks

Tips for Using dailyBooks Conversation Starters:

EVERY GOOD BOOK CONTAINS A WORLD FAR DEEPER THAN the surface of its pages. The characters and their world come alive through the words on the pages, yet the characters and its world still live on. Questions herein are designed to bring us beneath the surface of the page and invite us into the world that lives on. These questions can be used to:

- Foster a deeper understanding of the book
- Promote an atmosphere of discussion for groups
- Assist in the study of the book, either individually or corporately
- Explore unseen realms of the book as never seen before

About Us:

THROUGH YEARS OF EXPERIENCE AND FIELD EXPERTISE, from newspaper featured book clubs to local library chapters, *dailyBooks* can bring your book discussion to life. Host your book party as we discuss some of today's most widely read books.

Table of Contents

Introducing *The Sound of Glass*

THE SOUND OF GLASS TAKES PLACE BOTH IN THE present and the past. The three narrators of the story are Merritt Heyward, Edith Heyward, and Loralee Purvis Connors. The story centers around a 1950s plane crash, and the three women are all connected by it.

When the plane crash occurred, Edith was a witness to it. In the wreckage of the crash, Edith came upon a suitcase. She kept the suitcase hidden and never spoke a word of it to anyone. When she opened the suitcase, she found a letter that made her feel as though she was not alone and not the only person with a secret.

For years, Edith had endured her husband's physical abuse. Calhoun would often hit her and would never allow her to have a door locked. Calhoun was also a witness to the plane crash. The explosion distracted him and led to a car crash, which resulted in his death. Edith did not mourn. She did not feel heartbroken as he had broken her heart many times before. In fact, she felt freedom after her husband's death.

In the present-day section of the story, Merritt Heyward's husband Cal has just passed away. During the same time, Cal's grandmother Edith passed away as well, which left Merritt to inherit Edith's house in South Carolina. Merritt knew little about Cal's childhood because he refused to speak about it. She only knew that his parents had died, and he had a younger brother. Merritt was also secretive, keeping her past from Cal. She never told him how she no longer spoke to her father after he had left to marry a flight attendant who was only five years older than her.

Feeling as though there is nothing left for her in Maine, Merritt decides to live in Cal's grandmother's house, hoping to leave her life in Maine behind her. Soon after she arrives, her stepmother Loralee and her 10-year-old stepbrother Owen arrive on her doorstep looking for a place to live. Loralee was recently widowed as well. Merritt agrees to let them stay in the house. While living in the house, Merritt also gets to meet her brother-in-law, Dr. Gibbes Heyward, whom she loathes immediately after meeting.

Introducing the Author

THOUGH SHE WAS BORN IN TULSA, OKLAHOMA, KAREN White spent her childhood living in various locations in and outside of the United States, including Venezuela and England. After her graduation from The American School of London, she attended college in New Orleans, Louisiana, at Tulane University. At Tulane, White studied Management and earned her bachelor's degree in the subject. She also graduated with honors and worked in business for several years before the release of her first novel.

As a child, White's greatest inspiration was the story *Gone with the Wind*. White recalls skipping school so she could read the book. After finishing the book, she was stuck with the decision to become like Scarlett O'Hara or to pursue a writing career.

In 2000, White published her first book, *In the Shadow of the Moon,* which became a finalist to win The Romance Writers of America RITA Award. White has released a novel every year following her first publication in addition to writing a book series, The Tradd Street Series. Her 2009 novel, *The Girl on Legare Street,* found a place on *The New York Times* Best Seller list. Her most recent book release was *The Sound of Glass* in 2015. There is also a new book, *Flight Patterns,* set to be released in May 2016. White typically writes books set in the Southern United States. Her preferred genres to write in are "grit-lit" and contemporary mystery.

White currently lives near Atlanta, Georgia, with her husband and their two children. The family also has one dog named Quincy, who inspired a character in her Tradd Street series. For White, it is impossible to imagine a life without reading. A few of her favorite authors are Margaret Mitchell and Diana Gabaldon and tends to stay away from reading by authors who write in a similar genre as her. In addition to reading and writing, Karen White's other hobbies include making scrapbooks and playing the piano.

Discussion Questions

. . . .

question 1

Consider the plane crash that takes place in *The Sound of Glass*. How did the crash affect the town of Beaufort? How did it affect Edith, Merritt, and Loralee?

. . . .

. . . .

question 2

Edith had to keep many things a secret in *The Sound of Glass*
because of the abuse from her husband. Why do you think she
continued to keep these things a secret after her husband's
death?

. . . .

. . . .

question 3

In the story, Edith makes wind chimes out of sea glass. Why do
you think she does this? What do you think the wind chimes
represent?

. . . .

. . . .

question 4

Merritt feels guilty about her husband's death, and she blames
herself. Why do you think she blames herself for his death?

. . . .

. . . .

question 5

Throughout the story, Merritt makes many changes. She moves
to a new state after her husband's death and lives with her
stepmother and stepbrother. In what ways does Merritt
transform from the beginning to the end of this story?

. . . .

. . . .

question 6

Edith begins the story as an abused and secretive woman. How
does she change throughout the story?

. . . .

. . . .

question 7

When Loralee first goes to stay with Merritt, the two are not on good terms. Throughout the story, how does the relationship between these two women change?

. . . .

. . . .

question 8

Loralee goes to live with Merritt after her husband's death. What
personal journey does she go on throughout the novel? Is she
different at the end of the novel than when she first enters the
story?

. . . .

. . . .

question 9

All of the women in *The Sound of Glass* are connected by domestic violence. How does each woman deal with their tragic situations?

. . . .

. . . .

question 10

Merritt reads the "Beloved" letter. What the letter says and who it is written by is finally revealed. How did you feel about this reveal?

. . . .

. . . .

question 11

After reading the letter, Edith chose to keep the letter a secret.
Why do you think she chose to do this? Do you think it was right
to keep it a secret?

. . . .

. . . .

question 12

In *The Sound of Glass*, Loralee kept a Journal of Truths. Which
truth did you find resonated the most with you?

. . . .

. . . .

question 13

Secrecy is a theme in *The Sound of Glass*. Consider the secrets the characters keep. What do you think motivates them to keep their secrets?

. . . .

· ·

question 14

Merritt has a strong dislike for her late father and her stepmother
Loralee. Why do you think she decides to let Loralee and Owen
move in even though she does not like Loralee?

· ·

. . . .

question 15

The relationship between Merritt and Gibbes develops from
hatred of each other to a romantic relationship with each other.
How did you feel about their relationship?

. . . .

. . . .

question 16

A reader feels that Karen White is an excellent storyteller. What do you think about White's storytelling abilities?

. . . .

. . . .

question 17

One reader commented on Karen White's ability to tell a story at a good pace. In your opinion, how was White's pacing in the story?

. . . .

. . . .

question 18

The experience of living in South Carolina was easy to picture
while reading *The Sound of Glass*, according to another reader.
Did you find it easy to imagine the setting and characters in the
novel?

. . . .

. . . .

question 19

One reader stated that their favorite character was Loralee because of her resilience. Who was your favorite character in the novel and why?

. . . .

question 20

The Sound of Glass was described as sad and sentimental. How would you describe the tone of the story?

. . . .

question 21

One reader found it improbable that all of the characters were connected by domestic abuse and widowhood. Did you find the story plausible?

. . . .

. . . .

question 22

A few readers did not like the characters, and because of that,
found it difficult to read the story. What were your thoughts on
the characters?

. . . .

. . . .

question 23

Many readers said *The Sound of Glass* was a predictable story. Did you find yourself able to predict what was going to happen before it happened?

. . . .

. . . .

question 24

The Sound of Glass was enjoyed by many readers, and they could
not stop reading the story. Did you have a similar experience?

. . . .

. . . .

question 25

One reader stated that they were going to miss reading about the lives of the characters after completing the novel. How do you feel after reading the novel?

. . . .

question 26

Karen White has lived in several different countries. Do you think this influenced her perspective and writing in any way?

. . . .

question 27

Karen White studied management in college. How do you think
her education affects her writing career?

. . . .

. . . .

question 28

Karen White worked in business for many years before writing full-time. What do you think of her decision to work in another field before becoming a writer?

. . . .

· ·

question 29

Karen White has released at least one novel every year since the release of her first novel. Which of Whites books is your favorite and why?

· ·

· ·

question 30

Karen White chooses not to read books by authors who write in
the same genre as her. Why do you think she does this?

· ·

. . . .

question 31

In the story, Edith chooses to keep the contents of the suitcase a
secret. Would you have done the same?

. . . .

question 32

Merritt's husband Cal passes away. How might the story be different if Cal did not die and chose to move into his grandmother's house with Merritt?

. . . .

question 33

Loralee carries around her Journal of Truths in *The Sound of Glass*. If you were Loralee, what "truths" would you include in your own Journal of Truths?

. . . .

. . . .

question 34

Many of the characters in *The Sound of Glass* have secrets they keep. Have you ever had a secret to keep? How was the experience of keeping a secret?

. . . .

question 35

The suitcase is found by Edith in *The Sound of Glass*. How might the story be different if Merritt or Loralee had found the suitcase?

. . . .

question 36

If one day you came across a mysterious letter as Edith does in
The Sound of Glass, what would you do with the letter?

. . . .

. . . .

question 37

Merritt moves to South Carolina in the story. If she had not moved to South Carolina, how would the story be different?

. . . .

. . . .

question 38

After her husband and her husband's grandmother die, Merritt moves to South Carolina. If you were in Merritt's position, would you have made the move to a new state?

. . . .

Quiz Questions

. . . .

question 39

The Sound of Glass begins with a _____ in 1955. This event affected many of the characters in the novel.

. . . .

question 40

_____ has suffered abuse from her husband Calhoun for many years. Upon his death, she does not mourn him.

question 41

Edith finds a _____ in the wreckage of the plane crash. She decides to keep the contents of the suitcase a secret.

. . . .

question 42

Many years later, _____'s husband Cal has died. She
gets news that her husband's grandmother has recently passed
as well, and she is the rightful heir to her home.

. . . .

question 43

Merritt decides to move to South Carolina. As soon as she arrives there, her stepmother _____ shows up with her stepbrother.

question 44

Merritt also meets Cal's brother _____, whom she loathes as soon as she meets him. Eventually, the two reconcile their differences and enter a romantic relationship.

question 45

Edith, Merritt, and Loralee were not only all connected by the plane crash. They were also all victims of
_____.

question 46

Karen White, the author of *The Sound of Glass*, was born in
_____. However, she spent her childhood in
many different locations around the world.

question 47

Karen White attended Tulane University in Louisiana. While there, she studied _____ and worked in business before becoming an author.

question 48

In 2000, Karen White released her first novel, _____. She has released at least one book every year since 2000.

question 49

Most of Karen White's books take place in the
_____. She describes her writing
genre as "grit-lit" and contemporary mystery.

. . . .

question 50

Karen White currently lives in Atlanta, Georgia. Her hobbies outside of writing include making _____ and playing _____.

. . . .

Quiz Answers

1. Queenie
2. Maureen
3. postcard
4. False; Harold walks.
5. True
6. False; Harold does not go to visit Queenie.
7. True
8. England
9. actress
10. plays
11. *The Unlikely Pilgrimage of Harold Fry*
12. True

THE END

Want to promote your book group? Register here.

PLEASE LEAVE US A FEEDBACK.

THANK YOU!

Made in the USA
Middletown, DE
27 June 2023